Object Talks

on the Parables of Jesus
by Lois Edstrom

STANDARD PUBLISHING
Cincinnati, Ohio

2857

Illustrated by Richard Briggs

ISBN: 0-87239-721-1

Contents

The Lamp Under the Bowl

(Matthew 5:14-16)

Let your light shine before men, that they may see your good deeds and praise your Father in heaven. —*Matthew 5:16*

Object Needed: A T-shirt with a message written across the front (a spiritual message would be especially effective)

Many people like to wear T-shirts with something written across the front of the shirt. The writing may be a special slogan or expression that is important to the person wearing the shirt. It may be the name of a school, club, town, or state. The shirt may carry the name of a favorite football, basketball, baseball, or soccer team.

The shirt is used to *convey a message.* Whatever is written on the shirt is usually something of which the wearer is proud. The person wearing the shirt is telling others that he is a member of a certain club, attends a particular school, lives in or has visited the city or state mentioned. The message is a personal choice that says something about the owner. Others can learn something about a person by the shirt he chooses to wear. It is a way of letting people know what is important to you.

In the Bible, Jesus talked to His disciples about conveying a message. "You are the light of the world. A city on a hill cannot be hidden. Neither do people light a lamp and put it under a bowl. Instead they put it on its stand, and it gives light to everyone in the house. In the same way, let your light shine before men, that they may see your good deeds and praise your Father in heaven."

The instruction Jesus gave to the disciples is also good advice for us. We should live our lives in a way that people will know what is important to us. If God is at the center of our lives, His Spirit will be a part of us and be evident in the things we do. What we believe is shown to other people by what we do and say. It is something we feel good about and of which we are proud. His Spirit gives love, peace, and joy to other people. Our lives *convey a message* of our faith and trust in God.

The Weeds

(Matthew 13:24-30)

Let both grow together until the harvest.
—*Matthew 13:30*

Object Needed: Newspaper headlines

The large words found at the top of a story or an article in a newspaper are called a headline. The words are usually in large type and describe the article or story briefly.

Headlines can carry good news or bad news. Headlines that are fun to read may tell us about weddings, your home team's victories, interesting animals, good weather, or people who have done great things. They might also let us know about sales, concerts, or special events. Can you think of other examples of good headlines?

Headlines that carry bad news can make us feel sad or upset. They may inform us of automobile accidents, bad storms, or various crimes.

Although we wish that all news could be good news, we must realize that our world is a combination of good and bad influences. We should *be aware* that both exist so we can make good choices.

Jesus told "The Parable of the Weeds" to teach us about good and evil. "The kingdom of heaven is like a man who sowed good seed in his field. But while everyone was sleeping, his enemy came and sowed weeds among the wheat, and went away. When the wheat sprouted and formed heads, then the weeds also appeared.

"The owner's servants came to him and said, 'Sir, didn't you sow good seed in your field? Where then did the weeds come from?'

"'An enemy did this,' he replied.

"The servants asked him, 'Do you want us to go and pull them up?'

"'No,' he answered, 'because while you are pulling the weeds, you may root up the wheat with them. Let both grow together until the harvest. At that time I will tell the harvesters: First collect the weeds and tie them in bundles to be burned, then gather the wheat and bring it into my barn.'"

The disciples asked Jesus to explain the parable and He answered in this way: "The one who sowed the good seed is the Son of Man. The field is the world, and the good seed stands for the sons of the kingdom. The weeds are the sons of the evil one, and the enemy who sows them is the devil. The harvest is the end of the age, and the harvesters are angels" (Matthew 13:37-39).

The parable teaches us that God creates good people. Those who accept God's love and share it with others have useful, rewarding lives.

People who haven't accepted God's love may make bad choices that can be harmful to themselves and others. They may respond to the evil influences in our world.

Just as there are headlines that carry good news and bad news, we must *be aware* that there are people who make good choices and people who make bad choices. If we recognize the power of God's love and listen to the "Good News" as recorded in the Bible, we can feel hopeful and expect good things to happen. "Do not be overcome by evil, but overcome evil with good" (Romans 12:21).

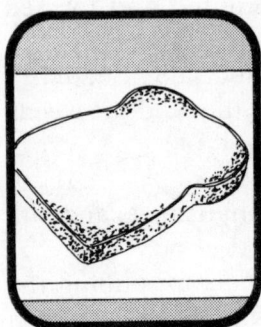

The Mustard Seed

(Matthew 13:31, 32)

Though it is the smallest of all your seeds, yet when it grows, it is the largest of garden plants and becomes a tree . . .

—*Matthew 13:32*

Object Needed: Moldy bread

Have you ever noticed a furry, bluish-green spot on bread? The spot, called mold, develops when bread becomes stale or damp.

In 1928, a scientist, Alexander Fleming, was studying bacteria when he noticed mold growing on one of his experiments. He watched the mold grow and realized that it gave off a liquid that destroyed the harmful bacteria he had been studying.

From a tiny speck of mold, similar to what you may find on bread, the wonder drug penicillin was discovered. This was one of the greatest achievements of all time. Before the discovery of penicillin, pneumonia was an illness that was very dangerous and could not be cured. Today, because of penicillin, pneumonia and many other diseases can be controlled and eliminated.

One of the things we can learn from this story is that *something very small can make big things happen.*

In the New Testament, Jesus Christ describes the kingdom of Heaven in a similar way. "The kingdom of heaven is like a mustard seed, which a man took and planted in his field. Though it is the smallest of all your seeds, yet when it grows, it is the largest of garden plants and becomes a tree, so that the birds of the air come and perch in its branches."

There are many things we don't understand about God and the kingdom of Heaven. Our faith, that part of us that believes in God, at times may seem very small. From a tiny

8

speck of faith we receive something very big—God's love. When we use God's love to understand and help others, *even our small faith can make big things happen.* Love and faith affect the way we live and have an effect on others. Faith grows and becomes powerful. Just as penicillin developed from a tiny, common mold and a small mustard seed grows into a large plant, so God's love, working through us, continues to expand and change lives.

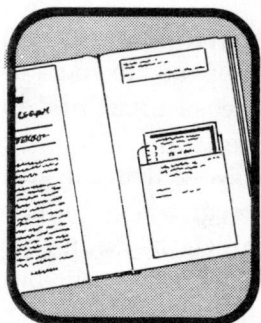

The Friend at Midnight

(Luke 11:5-12)

Ask and it will be given to you; seek and you will find; knock and the door will be opened to you.

—*Luke 11:9*

Objects Needed: Library books; library card

A library is an interesting place to visit. It offers many chances to learn. Its shelves are lined with hundreds of books. What fun it is to wander through the aisles and see what's there. The choices are endless.

Besides books, some libraries have pictures, records, and tapes that can be borrowed. Everyone may explore the library and select the things they want to use.

After you decide what you would like to borrow, what must you do? Tell the librarian! Gather the books, pictures, records, or tapes together and take them to the check-out counter. Some libraries require a library card and others use a sign-up sheet. When you present a library card or write your name on a sign-up sheet you are *asking* permission to use the items you have chosen. You are letting the librarian know what you want from the library.

Jesus talked to His disciples about a similar idea when

He told them the story of "The Friend at Midnight." He was teaching them about prayer and He said to them, "Suppose one of you has a friend, and he goes to him at midnight and says, 'Friend, lend me three loaves of bread, because a friend of mine on a journey has come to me, and I have nothing to set before him.'

"Then the one inside answers, 'Don't bother me. The door is already locked, and my children are with me in bed. I can't get up and give you anything.' I tell you, though he will not get up and give him the bread because he is his friend, yet because of the man's persistence he will get up and give him as much as he needs.

"So I say to you: Ask and it will be given to you; seek and you will find; knock and the door will be opened to you. For everyone who asks receives; he who seeks finds; and to him who knocks, the door will be opened.

"Which of you fathers, if your son asks for a fish, will give him a snake instead? Or if he asks for an egg will give him a scorpion? If you then, though you are evil, know how to give good gifts to your children, how much more will your Father in heaven give the Holy Spirit to those who ask him!"

In the parable of "The Friend at Midnight" the man asked a friend to give him bread. He made his needs known. He explained why he needed the bread and continued to ask until the bread was given. The friend gave him as much as he needed.

Prayer is a way of talking with our Heavenly Father. He is a friend. We must let Him know what we need and *ask* Him to take care of those needs. When we communicate with God through prayer, the opportunities and choices are endless. Because our Heavenly Father loves us He knows what is best for us. The Bible tells us that He longs to give us gifts that will enrich our lives. Those gifts are love, peace, and joy—the gifts of the Holy Spirit. "Ask and it will be given to you!"

The Yeast

(Matthew 13:33)

The kingdom of heaven is like yeast that a woman took and mixed into a large amount of flour until it worked all through the dough.
— *Matthew 13:33*

Object Needed: A tablespoon of baking soda in a tall glass; about ⅛ cup of vinegar

Let's talk about change. Change means to make something different or to give it a different form. A tablespoon of ordinary baking soda has been placed in a tall glass. As vinegar is added, notice what happens. *A change takes place!* The mixture, baking soda and vinegar, becomes frothy and fills the glass. The bubbles are formed by a gas called carbon dioxide. This dramatic reaction is the result of vinegar, an acid, neutralizing the baking soda, which is a base.

The carbon dioxide we watched being formed is the same ingredient that gives soda pop its fizz and causes cakes to rise.

When bread is baked a similar process takes place. Yeast, a tiny one-celled plant, is mixed with flour. When sugar and a warm liquid are added the yeast grows and bubbles of carbon dioxide are formed, causing the dough to change. The bread rises and becomes soft and light.

Jesus talked about yeast and what He said is recorded in the Bible. "The kingdom of heaven is like yeast that a woman took and mixed into a large amount of flour until it worked all through the dough."

God's love is the ingredient that causes *change to take place!* Just as yeast affects bread dough, God's love affects our lives. When we accept His love into our lives it becomes a part of us. It is the necessary ingredient that causes a reaction to take place. Love makes things happen! We may feel the change in many ways—joy, peace, patience, or kindness. Can you think of others? As we share God's love, it grows and affects other people. It is the power or force within us and around us in the world that makes things work in a dramatic way. "The kingdom of heaven is like this!"

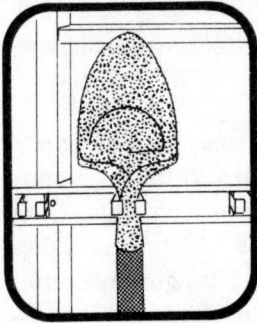

The Lost Sheep

(Luke 15:3-7)

There is more rejoicing in heaven over one sinner who repents than over ninety-nine righteous persons who do not need to repent.
—Luke 15:7

Objects Needed: Shovel; pictures of artifacts that have been found

An archaeologist is a person who digs for clues to the past. His main tool is a shovel and his job consists of digging through layers of dirt to find old pots, artwork, baskets, bones, coins, or tools. These objects, called artifacts, are *valuable* because they give clues to how people lived long ago.

When an archaeologist discovers something that has been *lost* for ages there is great excitement and *joy*. Often one small object can give useful information about the language or lifestyle of ancient people. Sometimes archaeologists even find part of a city, buried for thousands of years.

Because the artifacts are old, they are often fragile. The workers must be extremely careful so the treasure will not be broken or damaged. Sometimes it is necessary to sift dirt through a screen so small items will not be overlooked.

"The Parable of the Lost Sheep" is also about finding something that has been lost. Jesus used the parable to teach about salvation. "Suppose one of you has a hundred sheep and loses one of them. Does he not leave the ninety-nine in the open country and go after the lost sheep until he

12

finds it? And when he finds it, he joyfully puts it on his shoulders and goes home. Then he calls his friends and neighbors together and says, 'Rejoice with me; I have found my lost sheep.' I tell you that in the same way there is more rejoicing in heaven over one sinner who repents than over ninety-nine righteous persons who do not need to repent."

Each person is *valuable* to God. Without God's direction and love we are *lost*. He calls us to himself; when we answer, there is great *joy!*

The Net

(Matthew 13:47, 48)

The kingdom of heaven is like a net that was let down into the lake and caught all kinds of fish.

—Matthew 13:47

Object Needed: Sunshine, or the light in the room

Can you think of something that is seen and used by everyone? The sun! It is at the center of our solar system. The earth and other planets revolve around it. It is the closest and most important star. People, animals, and plants depend on the sun as a source of heat, light, and energy.

The sun is powerful! It is a ball of hot gases, many times larger than the earth. In its core, nuclear reactions take place that produce energy. The energy escapes to the surface of the sun and travels to earth where it warms the land, oceans, and air. (The temperature of the sun at its core is 27,000,000 degrees Fahrenheit.)

We can feel the sun's warmth on our bodies and see its beauty in the sunrise and sunset. We keep track of time by watching the sun. Sailors use the sun to find their position in the ocean. Hikers check directions by using the sun. The sun helps plants grow and produce food. It lights and warms the world!

All life on earth depends on the sun for survival. People in Africa, Asia, Antarctica, Australia, Europe, North and South America experience the benefits of the sun. *Everyone* is affected by the sun. It is available to all.

There is something else that is available to everyone. Jesus used "The Parable of the Net" to teach us about this idea. "Once again, the kingdom of heaven is like a net that was let down into the lake and caught all kinds of fish. When it was full, the fishermen pulled it up on the shore. Then they sat down and collected the good fish in baskets, but threw the bad away."

The kingdom of heaven is available to *everyone!* God's love, which like the sun is very powerful, is offered to all the people of the world. Just as all kinds of fish were caught in the fishermen's net, there are all kinds of people in our world. They live in many countries, speak different languages, and do various kinds of work. They can all experience the benefits of God's love.

God is at the center of the universe. He created us and our world. Accepting God's love is the most important thing we can do. Like the sun, God's love is a source or warmth, energy, and light for our lives. We use His love in the best way when we share it with others. The kingdom of Heaven is available to all. Take advantage of what is offered and use God's power to grow and find direction for your life. You can depend on it!

The Watchful Servants

(Luke 12:35-38)

It will be good for those servants whose master finds them ready.

—Luke 12:38

Objects Needed: Swimsuit, towel, beach bag, picnic food, and other items for the beach or pool

If a friend invited you to go to the beach, what would you take along?

The first thing you might want to pack would be a swimsuit, in case you were able to go swimming. You would need a towel to use after swimming and perhaps a bag to hold the gear. You might want a mat to lie on, food to eat, and something cold to drink. A beach ball or a Frisbee would also be fun to take along. Can you think of other things you would take to the beach?

An invitation to go to the beach is something to *look forward to* and it is best to *be prepared and ready for action!* Take responsibility to decide what is important and what you might need to have fun at the beach.

In the New Testament Christ told a story about making preparations. "Be dressed ready for service and keep your lamps burning, like men waiting for their master to return from a wedding banquet, so that when he comes and knocks they can immediately open the door for him. It will be good for those servants whose master finds them watching when he comes. I tell you the truth, he will dress himself to serve, will have them recline at the table and will come and wait on them. It will be good for those servants whose master finds them ready, even if he comes in the second or third watch of the night."

Often our lives get so busy that we forget to think about

15

God and our plans for the future. The story of "The Watchful Servants" reminds us that we should *be prepared and ready for action!* Just as it is a good idea to make plans for fun at the beach, so should we spend time thinking about God and His plan for our lives. We need to pray and listen for directions. We have a responsibility to decide what is important and what we should do to prepare ourselves to be a part of God's plan. We should think about how to live our lives in a way that is pleasing to God. His promise of eternal life is something to *look forward to!*

The Growing Seed

(Mark 4:26-29)

Night and day, whether he sleeps or gets up, the seed sprouts and grows, though he does not know how.

—*Mark 4:27*

Object Needed: Some ice cream, or a picture of an ice cream cone or sundae; an ice cream freezer and ingredients for making ice cream

Do you like ice cream? Almost everyone does. It is sweet, cold, and delicious.

We usually buy ice cream at the supermarket, but before refrigerators were invented, people made their own ice cream. Although refrigerators are now common, some people like to make ice cream the old-fashioned way. This is how it is done.

An ice cream freezer is needed. Cream, milk, sugar, and flavoring are placed in the metal container, which is inside a bucket. A mixing device that is turned by a handle is fastened on top of the bucket. By turning the handle the ice cream ingredients are mixed and frozen. As the mixture freezes the handle becomes harder to turn. After the ingredients are well mixed, more ice is packed around the container and it is covered with a towel. The ice cream must remain covered with ice until it is thoroughly frozen.

The most difficult part of making ice cream is waiting for it to be ready to be eaten. The process of making this good-tasting treat takes time. It cannot be rushed. One must have *patience* to make ice cream. If we are patient we will be rewarded with good results. The finished product, delicious ice cream, is worth the time and effort given.

"The Parable of the Growing Seed" teaches us about patience. Jesus said, "This is what the kingdom of God is like. A man scatters seed on the ground. Night and day, whether he sleeps or gets up, the seed sprouts and grows, though he does not know how. All by itself the soil produces grain—first the stalk, then the head, then the full kernel in the head. As soon as the grain is ripe, he puts the sickle to it, because the harvest has come."

A seed is planted in the ground and during the day and night, although we can't see it, a change is taking place within the seed. We can prepare the soil, water the seed, and remove weeds, but we can't make the seed grow. It grows at its own rate. Nothing we do can hurry its growth. We must have patience and know that the growth of the seed is God's work. The growth of a seed is slow and gradual but eventually there is a plant to be harvested.

Jesus tells us that the kingdom of God is like the growth of a seed. God's love is offered to everyone. When an individual accepts His love a change takes place within that person. The change is mysterious and we don't fully understand it because we can't see what happens. The important thing to remember is that God takes care of us and makes love grow.

Just as we must wait for ice cream to freeze and for a seed to grow, we must have *patience* to allow God's love to grow within us and within other people. God's love can change people and change the world!

The Two Debtors

(Luke 7:41-43)

Then Jesus said to her, "Your sins are forgiven." —Luke 7:48

Object Needed: A pizza, or pizza ingredients; cash register receipt

Have you ever gone to a pizza parlor and ordered pizza? First, you must decide how hungry you are so you know what size to order. Next, you need to decide if you want extra topping on the pizza. Cheese, olives, sausage, mushrooms, pepperoni, and bacon are some of the choices.

There is usually an additional charge for each topping that you choose. If you are very hungry and you order the largest pizza with all the extra toppings on it, you will need more money than if you had ordered the smallest pizza with one or two toppings.

How would you feel if you ordered the largest pizza with all the extra toppings and a friend came by and paid your bill? That would be a wonderful surprise! You would probably feel *gratitude* toward your friend and say thanks!

The parable of "The Two Debtors" is a story about *gratitude.* "Two men owed money to a certain moneylender. One owed him five hundred denarii, and the other fifty. Neither of them had the money to pay him back, so he canceled the debts of both. Now which of them will love him more?"

Simon replied, "I suppose the one who had the bigger debt canceled."

"You have judged correctly," Jesus said.

We all make mistakes, and we all do wrong things sometimes. It is impossible to go through life without making mistakes. Sometimes our sins are small; sometimes they are more serious. We might hurt ourselves or other people,

18

accidentally or on purpose. Our sins pile up like debts that can't be paid. We may accumulate many sins and wonder how to get rid of them.

God is like the moneylender who canceled the debts of the two men who owed him money. He has offered to cancel our debt of sin, if we ask for forgiveness. If we accept His love and forgiveness, we will feel *gratitude* and want to find ways to show our appreciation and thanks. God's great love gives us the freedom to love and serve Him!

The Sower

(Mark 4:3-9, 13-20)

Others, like seed sown on good soil, hear the word, accept it, and produce a crop— thirty, sixty, or even a hundred times what was sown.

—Mark 4:20

Object Needed: A tape recorder

(Ask each child to share something—for example, a way he would show love to others—and record their voices.)

A tape recorder has many uses! Business people use tape recorders to dictate letters. Students use tape recorders in the classroom to help them with their studies. Music can be recorded on a tape recorder to be enjoyed later. Tape recorders are used to get satellite signals from space.

Let's think about how a tape recorder works. A thin magnetic ribbon is threaded into the recorder. Sound waves enter a microphone and are changed into electric signals. The electric waves cause magnetic particles on the ribbon to line up in sound patterns. The sound patterns are stored on the ribbon for future use.

Understanding how a tape recorder works is difficult, but the thing to remember is that a recorder is valuable because it can *collect, store,* and play back *useful* information.

"The Parable of the Sower" is a story about collecting, storing, and using seeds. "A farmer went out to sow his seed. As he was scattering the seed, some fell along the path, and the birds came and ate it up. Some fell on rocky places, where it did not have much soil. It sprang up quickly, because the soil was shallow. But when the sun came up, the plants were scorched, and they withered because they had no root. Other seed fell among thorns, which grew up and choked the plants, so that they did not bear grain. Still other seed fell on good soil. It came up, grew and produced a crop, multiplying thirty, sixty, or even a hundred times."

Jesus explained the parable in this way: "The farmer sows the word. Some people are like seed along the path, where the word is sown. As soon as they hear it, Satan comes and takes away the word that was sown in them. Others, like seed sown on rocky places, hear the word and at once receive it with joy. But since they have no root, they last only a short time. When trouble or persecution comes because of the word, they quickly fall away. Still others, like seed sown among thorns, hear the word; but the worries of this life, the deceitfulness of wealth and the desires for other things come in and choke the word, making it unfruitful. Others, like seed sown on good soil, hear the word, accept it, and produce a crop—thirty, sixty, or even a hundred times what was sown."

What we can learn from thinking about a tape recorder and "The Parable of the Sower" is that we need to *collect* information about God. We can do this by studying the Bible, talking with others, and praying. To grow from the information we collect, we must *store* it inside and think about it. If we *use* what we learn about God to be helpful and kind to others, God's love will multiply.

(At the end of the lesson, play back the recording.)

The Talents

(Matthew 25:14-30)

For everyone who has will be given more, and he will have an abundance.
—*Matthew 25:29*

Objects Needed: A lock and key; a collection of keys to show the unique shape of each one

Have you ever thought about how a key opens a lock? Each key has a unique shape and will only fit the lock that has been designed for it.

If you have a key for your house you know that your key will open the door. The correct key must be placed in the lock in the right way. It will not turn or open the lock if it is inserted upside down.

When the correct key is put into the lock the right way, the grooves on the key match up with metal pins inside the lock and allow the key to turn.

The important thing to remember about keys is that to open a door a key must be *used in the right way*. If you were afraid of losing your key, kept it in your pocket and didn't use it, it would have no value.

"The Parable of the Talents" is a story about how action gets results. "Again, it will be like a man going on a journey, who called his servants and entrusted his property to them. To one he gave five talents of money, to another two talents, and to another one talent, each according to his ability. Then he went on his journey. The man who had received the five talents went at once and put his money to work and gained five more. So also, the one with the two talents gained two more. But the man who had received the one talent went off, dug a hole in the ground and hid his master's money.

"After a long time the master of those servants returned and settled accounts with them. The man who had received the five talents brought the other five. 'Master,' he said, 'you entrusted me with five talents. See, I have gained five more.'

"His master replied, 'Well done, good and faithful servant! You have been faithful with a few things; I will put you in charge of many things. Come and share your master's happiness!'

"The man with the two talents also came. 'Master,' he said, 'you entrusted me with two talents; see, I have gained two more.'

"His master replied, 'Well done, good and faithful servant! You have been faithful with a few things; I will put you in charge of many things. Come and share your master's happiness!'

"Then the man who had received the one talent came. 'Master,' he said, 'I knew that you are a hard man, harvesting where you have not sown and gathering where you have not scattered seed. So I was afraid and went out and hid your talent in the ground. See, here is what belongs to you.'

"His master replied, 'You wicked, lazy servant! So you knew that I harvest where I have not sown and gather where I have not scattered seed? Well then, you should have put my money on deposit with the bankers, so that when I returned I would have received it back with interest.

" 'Take the talent from him and give it to the one who has the ten talents.' "

God has given each of us special talents and abilities. Just as each key has a different shape, each of us has a different skill. One person may be a good cook, another a builder, another a painter of beautiful pictures.

"The Parable of the Talents" teaches us that we have a responsibility to use these unique gifts. Just as a key must be used to open a door, we must *use our special talents and abilities in the right way.* There must be action to get results. When we make good use of what God has given us we increase our value to ourselves and others.

Take advantage of what God gives you—use your talents!

The Pharisee and the Tax Collector

(Luke 18:9-14)

> For everyone who exalts himself will be humbled, and he who humbles himself will be exalted.
>
> — Luke 18:14

Object Needed: A small stepladder, to sit on while talking to the children

A ladder is useful if you need to wash windows, paint the house, or get a Frisbee off the roof. A small stepladder is convenient for getting cookies from a high cupboard or changing a light bulb.

What happens when you climb a ladder? You put *yourself above others.* It would be awkward if I sat on the top of a ladder while we talked. We would find it difficult to communicate. If you put yourself above other people, you put distance between yourself and them.

The view from the top of a ladder is different. You *look down on others.* It is difficult to know a person if your view is of the top of his head.

Ladders are helpful when used in the right way, but they can be dangerous if misused. A ladder must be placed so that it is stable or it could become unbalanced and tip.

God puts people on the same level. He offers His love to everyone! It is not necessary to *put ourselves above others* by feeling that we are better. We should not *look down on others* by pointing out their faults. If we become self-righteous it is easy to lose our balance. Self-righteous people find it difficult to communicate because they put themselves above others.

In "The Parable of the Pharisee and the Tax Collector" Christ shows us an example of a man who was self-righteous. "Two men went up to the temple to pray, one a Pharisee and the other a tax collector. The Pharisee stood up and prayed about himself: 'God, I thank you that I am not like all other men—robbers, evildoers, adulterers—or even like this tax collector. I fast twice a week and give a tenth of all I get.'

"But the tax collector stood at a distance. He would not even look up to heaven, but beat his breast and said, 'God, have mercy on me, a sinner.'

"I tell you that this man, rather than the other, went home justified before God."

We all have value to God. We need to look at ourselves and others clearly. No person is above another in receiving God's love and forgiveness!

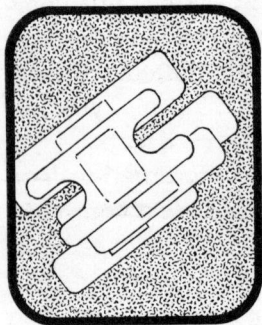

The Unmerciful Servant

(Matthew 18:21-35)

"Shouldn't you have had mercy on your fellow servant just as I had on you?"
—*Matthew 18:33*

Object Needed: Band-Aids or other types of bandages

Have you ever scraped your knee or cut your finger? What did you do to make it feel better? Perhaps you washed your wound and put a Band-Aid on it. A Band-Aid covers the wound, protects it, and keeps it clean so it can heal faster.

Sometimes people get hurt in a different way. When we feel jealous, angry, or unkind we may say or do something that can hurt ourselves and other people. We feel that kind of hurt inside, and it can't be helped by a Band-Aid.

When we know we have made a bad choice and hurt ourselves or others, *forgiveness* is the only thing that can help heal the hurt we feel or have caused. God's love covers the hurt and allows us to heal.

Christ was asked about forgiveness, and He answered by telling this story. "Therefore, the kingdom of heaven is like a king who wanted to settle accounts with his servants. As he began the settlement, a man who owed him ten thousand talents (several million dollars) was brought to him. Since he was not able to pay, the master ordered that he and his wife and his children and all that he had be sold to repay the debt.

"The servant fell on his knees before him. 'Be patient with me,' he begged, 'and I will pay back everything.' The servant's master took pity on him, canceled the debt and let him go.

"But when that servant went out, he found one of his fellow servants who owed him a hundred denarii (a few dollars). He grabbed him and began to choke him. 'Pay back what you owe me!' he demanded.

"His fellow servant fell to his knees and begged him, 'Be patient with me, and I will pay you back.'

"But he refused. Instead, he went off and had the man thrown into prison until he could pay the debt. When the other servants saw what had happened, they were greatly distressed and went and told their master everything that had happened.

"Then the master called the servant in. 'You wicked servant,' he said. 'I canceled all that debt of yours because you begged me to. Shouldn't you have had mercy on your fellow servant just as I had on you?' In anger his master turned him over to the jailers until he should pay back all he owed.

"This is how my heavenly Father will treat each of you unless you forgive your brother from your heart."

God's love is so great that if we ask Him, we will receive *forgiveness* for all the mistakes we have made and the hurts we have caused. The parable teaches us to use His love to forgive others. Forgiveness covers any wound and makes us and others feel better!

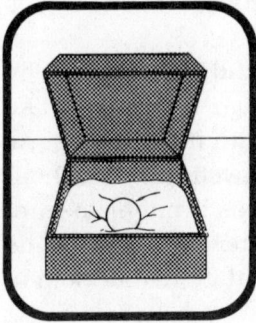

The Pearl

(Matthew 13:45, 46)

The kingdom of heaven is like a merchant looking for fine pearls. When he found one of great value, he went away and sold everything he had and bought it.   —*Matthew 13:45, 46*

Object Needed: Pearl jewelry, or a shell lined with mother-of-pearl

A pearl is not only *beautiful and valuable* but is different than other gems because of the way it is formed. Most gems are dug from the earth, cut into beautiful shapes, and polished. A pearl is produced by a living creature!

A pearl oyster is a soft-bodied underwater animal covered with a hard shell. The shell is lined with a substance that protects the soft body of the oyster from the hard surface of the shell. The substance is called nacre or mother-of-pearl. When a foreign object, such as a grain of sand, enters the shell the oyster protects itself by secreting the pearly material. The mother-of-pearl forms circular layers around the grain of sand and a pearl is formed. The pearl has a smooth, satiny appearance and may be white, cream, pink, or black.

Large natural pearls are rare. They are found in pearl oysters that lie on the sea bottom and must be gathered by divers. These beautiful gems increase in value depending on their size, shape, color, luster, and absence of blemishes. Many years ago, before men learned how to cut and polish other gems, the pearl was more highly prized.

Jesus used "The Parable of the Pearl" to describe the kingdom of Heaven. "Again, the kingdom of heaven is like a merchant looking for fine pearls. When he found one of great value, he went away and sold everything he had and bought it."

We, like people who search for pearls, must search for understanding about God. We can learn about God and His plan for our lives through prayer and by studying the Bible. A minister, our family, or our friends will also be able to answer some of our questions. As we understand more about God's Son, Jesus Christ, and accept His love, we receive the greatest gift of all—eternal life. When we realize the value of God's love, He becomes important to us and we are willing to give Him priority in our lives. The "kingdom of Heaven" is God's love working in us. We can find joy by putting God above all else. The kingdom of Heaven is worth the search. God's love, like a pearl, is *beautiful and valuable!*

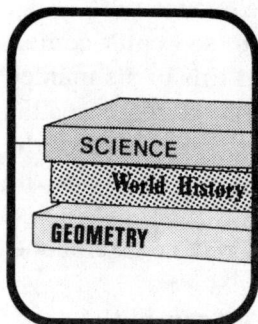

The Great Banquet

(Luke 14:15-24)

Come, for everything is now ready.
—*Luke 14:17*

Object Needed: Textbooks; a written excuse

When you miss a day at school, the principal usually wants a note from your parents explaining why you were absent. The note may read, "Ann was absent yesterday because she had the flu." Illness makes an absence necessary.

If you decided to stay home and watch television, go shopping, or ride your bike when you should be at school, you would miss out on everything school has to offer. Books full of artwork, stories, and instruction are available. A gymnasium to use for exercise and fun is often provided. Teachers study, prepare themselves to teach, and are eager to share what they have learned. Friends are an important part of a school day.

School is *available to all children. Everything is ready* for students who want to learn. Those who go to school regularly benefit from what it offers. Those who find *excuses* for not going to school miss the opportunity to grow and develop.

Jesus used "The Parable of the Great Banquet" to teach people about making good choices. "A certain man was preparing a great banquet and invited many guests. At the time of the banquet he sent his servant to tell those who had been invited, 'Come for everything is now ready.'

"But they all alike began to make excuses. The first said, 'I have just bought a field, and I must go and see it. Please excuse me.'

"Another said, 'I have just bought five yoke of oxen, and I'm on my way to try them out. Please excuse me.'

"Still another said, 'I just got married, so I can't come.'

"The servant came back and reported this to his master. Then the owner of the house became angry and ordered his servant, 'Go out quickly into the streets and alleys of the town and bring in the poor, the crippled, the blind and the lame.'

" 'Sir,' the servant said, 'what you ordered has been done, but there is still room.'

"Then the master told his servant, 'Go out to the roads and the country lanes and make them come in, so that my house will be full. I tell you, not one of those men who were invited will get a taste of my banquet.' "

God's love is *available to everyone.* He invites all of us to be a part of His family. Some people make excuses and refuse God's love. We must decide what is important to us and make good choices. If we accept His invitation we will grow and benefit from the love that is offered.

Don't miss a good opportunity!

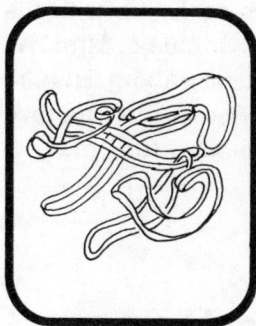

The Shepherd and His Flock

(John 10:1-6)

> . . . his sheep follow him because they know
> his voice. *—John 10:4*

Object Needed: Rubber band

We use our voices to let others know about our thoughts and feelings. We talk, sing, laugh, and cry. Have you ever thought about how the sound of your voice is produced? It is a remarkable process!

Located in your throat is a larynx, commonly called a voice box. Stretched across the voice box are two small bands of tissue—vocal cords (stretch the rubber band). Air from your lungs goes through the voice box and causes the vocal cords to vibrate, producing sound. As muscles pull the vocal cords tight a higher sound is made and when the cords are relaxed the sound is a lower pitch (pluck the rubber band at different lengths, to show how the pitch changes). Your tongue, lips, and teeth help shape the sounds that come out of your mouth.

When we spend time and get to know a person well, that person's voice becomes *familiar* to us. We learn to recognize the voice when we hear it. The voice of someone we love brings us comfort and joy. Because of love and friendship, we develop *trust* and respond to the familiar voice.

In the story of "The Shepherd and His Flock," Christ talks about a shepherd; he knows his sheep well, and they know him. "The man who enters by the gate is the shepherd of his sheep. The watchman opens the gate for him, and the sheep listen to his voice. He calls his own sheep by name and leads them out. When he has brought out all his own, he goes on ahead of them, and his sheep follow him because they know his voice."

29

Christ is like a shepherd who knows each sheep in his flock. We are separate, well-known individuals to Him. As we become *familiar* with Christ and learn about His life and purpose, we find comfort and joy. Because of His love and friendship we develop *trust* and respond to Him.

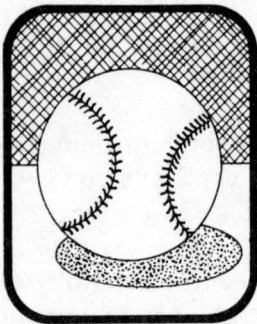

The Two Sons

(Matthew 21:28-32)

> Do not merely listen to the word, and so deceive yourselves. Do what it says.
> —*James 1:22*

Objects Needed: A baseball, bat, and glove

Have you ever played baseball? It can be exciting and fun! Baseball is a popular sport in the United States. Millions of people play baseball, listen to games on the radio, watch their favorite team on television, or visit a baseball park to see a game.

The batter steps up to the plate, lifts the bat, and waits for the pitcher to throw the ball. When the ball leaves the pitcher's glove, the batter is ready to swing.

To be a good hitter a baseball player must learn how to *follow through*. He must decide to swing at the ball, use good form, put energy into the swing, and follow through. A batter who uses this technique will be powerful and effective.

"The Parable of the Two Sons" is a story about *following through*. "What do you think?" Jesus asked the chief priests and elders of the temple. "There was a man who had two sons. He went to the first and said, 'Son, go and work today in the vineyard.'

"'I will not,' he answered, but later he changed his mind and went.

"Then the father went to the other son and said the same thing. He answered, 'I will, sir,' but he did not go.

"Which of the two did what his father wanted?"

"The first," they answered.

The parable explains the importance of doing what we say we will do. Our love for God is shown by the way we live our lives and treat others. We must decide to have faith in God, put energy into doing His work, and receive power from His love.

If we are honest and try to live according to God's commandments, people will know they can trust and depend on us. When we *follow through* and use His love we will be effective and powerful!

The Good Samaritan

(Luke 10:25-37)

Love your neighbor as yourself.
—*Matthew 10:27*

Object Needed: Some chocolate chip cookies; if situation permits, make cookies with the children

Have you ever baked chocolate chip cookies for someone? I don't know of anyone who doesn't like them. They are especially good when they are warm and the chocolate is soft and sweet.

There are many ways to be kind to other people. Baking cookies for someone is one way to show *kindness*.

To bake cookies the necessary ingredients should be assembled. You must follow the directions on the recipe and mix the ingredients in the right order. Next, the dough is placed on a cookie sheet that has been greased. When the temperature of the oven is just right the cookies are baked for ten to twelve minutes. After the cookies are baked they may be arranged on a plate to be given as a gift. It takes time to bake cookies, and that is what makes the gift so special! When you take the time and energy to bake cookies for someone you give not only cookies but a part of yourself.

In "The Parable of the Good Samaritan" Christ teaches us about kindness. "A man was going down from Jerusalem to Jericho, when he fell into the hands of robbers. They stripped him of his clothes, beat him and went away, leaving him half dead. A priest happened to be going down the same road, and when he saw the man, he passed by on the other side. So too, a Levite, when he came to the place and saw him, passed by on the other side. But a Samaritan, as he traveled, came where the man was; and when he saw him, he took pity on him. He went to him and bandaged his wounds, pouring on oil and wine. Then he put the man on his own donkey, took him to an inn and took care of him. The next day he took out two silver coins and gave them to the innkeeper. 'Look after him,' he said, 'and when I return, I will reimburse you for any extra expense you may have.'"

The Samaritan didn't know the man he found by the road but he cared about him. He showed *kindness* for the man by taking the time to help him.

Christ's life was an example of love, care, and concern for others. Christ finished the story of "The Good Samaritan" by saying, "Go and do likewise."

With God's love we can be helpful and caring to other people. We can use our time and energy to show *kindness* in many ways.

The Good Shepherd

(John 10:7-18)

I am the good shepherd. The good shepherd lays down his life for the sheep.
—*John 10:11*

Object Needed: Picture of an astronaut that shows the various parts of a space suit.

An astronaut is a man of strength and courage. When he travels in space he must wear special clothing for *protection* from the harmful conditions of space. In addition to a space suit, the astronaut wears a helmet with visor, gloves, and boots.

The space suit is made of strong material and is flexible so the astronaut can move around easily. It is airtight and pressurized. It has its own air and water supply. The temperature of the suit can be controlled to keep the astronaut comfortable. A microphone is also available so the space traveler can communicate with other astronauts and people on earth. The space suit is designed to protect and *take care of the needs* of the astronaut while he is in space.

The story of "The Good Shepherd" is a parable about *protection.* Jesus said, "I am the good shepherd. The good shepherd lays down his life for the sheep. The hired hand is not the shepherd who owns the sheep. So when he sees the wolf coming, he abandons the sheep and runs away. Then the wolf attacks the flock and scatters it. The man runs away because he is a hired hand and cares nothing for the sheep."

But the good shepherd loves and cares for his sheep, even to the extent of laying down his own life. We are like sheep, and Jesus is our Good Shepherd. "The reason my Father loves me is that I lay down my life—only to take it up again. No one takes it from me, but I lay it down of my own accord. I have authority to lay it down and authority to take it up again. This command I received from my Father."

A shepherd, like an astronaut, is a man of strength and courage. He *provides for the needs* of his flock. Jesus describes himself as "the good shepherd" who is willing to die to protect the sheep from the wolf. Just as a shepherd knows his sheep and cares for them, Jesus knows us and cares for us. His love for us is so great that He was willing to die for us. We are protected by His love. Just as sheep are gathered into one flock, with one shepherd, we are gathered into one church with Jesus Christ as our guide.

The Hidden Treasure

(Matthew 13:44)

The kingdom of heaven is like treasure hidden in a field. When a man found it, he hid it again, and then in his joy went and sold all he had and bought that field. — *Matthew 13:44*

Objects Needed: Coins, jewelry, or other objects thought of as treasure; pictures of pirates, treasure chests, or sailing ships

What do you think of when you hear the word *treasure?* Pirates, treasure chests, and sailing ships might come to mind. Pirates were robbers who seized ships and stole the treasure that was aboard. They often buried the jewels and gold in a secret place. There are still people today who search for hidden treasure.

Have you ever seen a person using a metal detector? By running a metal detector over the ground one is able to tell if a metal object is buried below. Coins, rings, watches, or pocket knives are some of the things that can be found.

Divers search for treasure under water. They locate sunken ships and explore the remains, looking for valuable items.

Maybe you have played a treasure hunt game. One person hides the treasure and places clues for others to find. The players must use the clues to figure out where the treasure is hidden. The treasure may be a toy or something the children will enjoy.

We can define treasure as something that is valuable. If the treasure is a collection of valuable things it is called a treasure trove. Exploring for hidden treasure is an exciting adventure. It can lead to thrilling discoveries!

Jesus used the example of "The Parable of the Hidden Treasure" to teach us about the value of God's love. "The kingdom of heaven is like treasure hidden in a field. When a man found it, he hid it again, and then in his joy went and sold all he had and bought that field."

The kingdom of God is described as "treasure hidden in a field." Learning about God and the possibilities that are offered to us is an exciting adventure. We learn that God loves us in a special way. His love is unconditional, a word that means He loves us just the way we are.

The Bible tells us that when we accept God's love, He sends the Holy Spirit to teach and comfort us. The gifts of the Holy Spirit are like a treasure trove—love, joy, and peace.

When we experience love, joy, and peace we want to share our treasure trove with others. The Scriptures assure us that each person has a special talent. We must develop our talents and search for ways to use our abilities to glorify God and help others.

By accepting God's love we experience joy. We are given gifts of great value. Like the man who sold everything he had to buy the field that held the buried treasure, Christians are willing to give priority to God. The kingdom of Heaven is like hidden *treasure,* waiting to be found. Searching for God's purpose for our lives leads to exciting discoveries!

The Wise and Foolish Builders

(Matthew 7:24-27)

Everyone who hears these words of mine and puts them into practice is like a wise man . . . — *Matthew 7:24*

Objects Needed: Various kinds of puppets

Puppets have been enjoyed by people around the world for thousands of years. Puppets were even found in ancient Egyptian tombs; today the most famous puppets are the Muppets.

How would you describe a puppet? A puppet is a small man-made figure of a person or an animal. It often has a cloth body and a hollow head. It can be a hand puppet, finger puppet, or a rod puppet. A puppet that is moved by strings is called a marionette. In all cases, a puppet is controlled by a person who makes the puppet move and perform. The person must also talk for the puppet.

Putting on a puppet show can be great fun because one can make the puppets, write the script, and use the puppets to entertain other people.

The unique thing about a puppet is that it must do what the person controlling it decides it will do. It says only what the person decides it will say. Because a puppet has no *choices* or *power*, it has no *wisdom*.

Christ told a story that is recorded in the New Testament about "The Wise and Foolish Builders." It is a lesson about choices, power, and wisdom. Christ said, "Therefore everyone who hears these words of mine and puts them into practice is like a wise man who built his house on the rock. The rain came down, the streams rose, and the winds blew and beat against that house; yet it did not fall, because it had its foundation on the rock. But everyone who hears these words of mine and does not put them into practice is

36

like a foolish man who built his house on sand. The rain came down, the streams rose, and the winds blew and beat against that house, and it fell with a great crash."

We hear God's words by studying the Bible, talking with others, and through prayer. As we learn more about God's plan for our lives, unlike the puppets, we have choices to make. According to the Bible, the best choice is to listen and accept God's love and wisdom. The wisdom that He gives helps us to make good choices and decisions. The story teaches us that if we decide to listen to God's words and try to live by them we will be given *wisdom* to make the right *choices*. Lives that are centered on Christ have strength and *power!*

The Lowest Seat at the Feast

(Luke 14:7-11)

For everyone who exalts himself will be humbled, and he who humbles himself will be exalted.   —*Luke 14:11*

Objects Needed: A raw egg and a hard-boiled egg; a tray

Let's conduct an experiment! Two eggs are needed for this test. The eggs are the same size, shape, and color. They seem identical. Let's place one of the eggs on a tray and twirl it. As you can see, it spins easily.

Now, let's do the same thing with the other egg. It spins slowly, in an irregular fashion, and soon stops. How are the two eggs different?

One egg is hard-boiled and the other is raw. Can you tell which one has been cooked? The raw egg is filled with liquid that moves around when the egg is twirled. As the

37

liquid moves, it slows the motion of the egg. The egg that has been cooked has a solid center and is able to spin easily. The eggs have a similar appearance. From the outside we can't tell the difference. *It's what is inside that makes the difference!* We can learn more about this idea by studying "The Parable of the Lowest Seat at the Feast."

When Jesus noticed how the guests picked the places of honor at the table, He told them this parable. "When someone invites you to a wedding feast, do not take the place of honor, for a person more distinguished than you may have been invited. If so, the host who invited both of you will come and say to you, 'Give this man your seat.' Then, humiliated, you will have to take the least important place. But when you are invited, take the lowest place, so that when your host comes, he will say to you, 'Friend, move up to a better place.' Then you will be honored in the presence of all your fellow guests. For everyone who exalts himself will be humbled, and he who humbles himself will be exalted."

At the time this parable was told, it was a custom for guests to be seated at a dinner in order of their importance and the host would decide who would be given a place of honor. At this particular feast, the guests were being selfish and trying to seat themselves in the best places. Jesus used the example of their behavior to teach about having the right attitude toward God and others.

It is not necessary for us to brag about our accomplishments and our importance. *It is what is inside that makes the difference!* Because Jesus is God, He is perfect. We can never be perfect and we don't need to be, because He accepts and loves us as we are. He sees our value and knows what we feel inside. When we give God a place of importance in our lives we are able to think of the needs of others. It is through service to God and others that we find honor. With God's love we are able to have a good attitude about ourselves and others!

The Workers in the Vineyard

(Matthew 20:1-16)

So the last will be first, and the first will be
last.   —*Matthew 20:16*

Objects Needed: An orange, orange marmalade, or candied orange peel; a bowl of various fruits.

An orange is a good fruit to pack in a lunch sack. It has its own wrapper, and when the peel is removed the fruit is sweet, juicy, good tasting, and fragrant.

Oranges were grown in China over two thousand years before Christ was born, but orange trees didn't grow in America until Christopher Columbus brought orange seeds here on one of his voyages. Today, most of the oranges grown in the United States are grown in Florida.

Oranges can be eaten as a fruit or made into orange juice, marmalade, or candied orange peel. Oil from the orange is made into flavorings and used in perfumes.

As wonderful as an orange is, we also have other fruits, berries, and melons. Apples, bananas, grapes, watermelons, peaches, strawberries, plums, and pears. Can you think of others?

When God created our world He was very generous. All around us, in many ways, we can see His *generosity* displayed. Instead of one kind of fruit we have many—all with different shapes, colors, and flavors. He has given us many things to appreciate and enjoy. Millions of stars, different kinds of animals, flowers in abundance, and huge seas. Can you think of other ways we can see God's generosity?

"The Parable of the Workers in the Vineyard" is also about *generosity*. When Jesus was talking to His disciples He told a story about "a landowner who went out early in the morning to hire men to work in his vineyard. He agreed

39

to pay them a denarius for the day and sent them into his vineyard.

"About the third hour he went out and saw others standing in the marketplace doing nothing. He told them, 'You also go and work in my vineyard, and I will pay you whatever is right.' So they went.

"He went out again about the sixth hour and the ninth hour and did the same thing. About the eleventh hour he went out and found still others standing around. He asked them, 'Why have you been standing here all day long doing nothing?'

"'Because no one has hired us,' they answered.

"'He said to them, 'You also go and work in my vineyard.'

"When evening came, the owner of the vineyard said to his foreman, 'Call the workers and pay them their wages, beginning with the last ones hired and going on to the first.'

"The workers who were hired about the eleventh hour came and each received a denarius. So when those came who were hired first, they expected to receive more. But each one of them also received a denarius. When they received it, they began to grumble against the landowner. 'These men who were hired last worked only one hour,' they said, 'and you have made them equal to us who have borne the burden of the work and the heat of the day.'

"But he answered one of them, 'Friend, I am not being unfair to you. Didn't you agree to work for a denarius? Take your pay and go. I want to give the man who was hired last the same as I gave you. Don't I have the right to do what I want with my own money? Or are you envious because I am generous?' "

The owner of the vineyard didn't have to pay the men that were hired late in the day as much as he gave the other workers. He did so because *he was generous.*

God has given us much more than we could ever ask for—not because we deserve it, but because of His great love for us. The parable reminds us not to compare what we have with that of others. We are to accept, appreciate, and enjoy God's generosity and be generous to others!

The Lost Son

(Luke 15:11-24)

We had to celebrate and be glad, because this brother of yours was dead and is alive again; he was lost and is found. — *Luke 15:31*

Object Needed: A well-mannered pet, or pictures of pets

Do you own a pet? Do you have friends who own pets? Perhaps you know what it feels like to love an animal. It may be a cat, dog, guinea pig, rabbit, bird, or fish. Pets give their owners love and companionship. They are interesting and fun.

Having a pet requires responsibility. A person must be willing to give his pet good care. An animal must have food, fresh water, and a place to sleep. Some animals need to have their coats brushed and groomed, and an occasional bath. All animals need love!

When a person spends time caring for an animal, his love for the animal grows. He and his pet begin to understand and respond to one another. The owner might feel concern and sadness if the pet becomes ill, and he will try to find a way to make the animal feel better. If a pet misbehaves, its master still loves it and takes care of it. A good pet owner loves and cares for the animal no matter what.

If someone you love gets hurt or suffers in any way, you may share that hurt and want to do something to help. That feeling is called *compassion.*

"The Parable of the Lost Son" is a story about compassion. "There was a man who had two sons. The younger one said to his father, 'Father, give me my share of the estate.' So he divided his property between them.

"Not long after that, the younger son got together all he had, set off for a distant country and there squandered his wealth in wild living. After he had spent everything, there

41

was a severe famine in that whole country, and he began to be in need. So he went and hired himself out to a citizen of that country, who sent him to his fields to feed pigs. He longed to fill his stomach with the pods that the pigs were eating, but no one gave him anything.

"When he came to his senses, he said, 'How many of my father's hired men have food to spare, and here I am starving to death! I will set out and go back to my father and say to him: Father, I have sinned against heaven and against you. I am no longer worthy to be called your son; make me like one of your hired men.' So he got up and went to his father.

"But while he was still a long way off, his father saw him and was filled with compassion for him; he ran to his son, threw his arms around him and kissed him.

"The son said to him, 'Father I have sinned against heaven and against you. I am no longer worthy to be called your son.'

"But the father said to his servants, 'Quick! Bring the best robe and put it on him. Put a ring on his finger and sandals on his feet. Bring the fattened calf and kill it. Let's have a feast and celebrate. For this son of mine was dead and is alive again; he was lost and is found.' So they began to celebrate."

The youngest son made some bad choices. He used all his wealth living in a way that was not good for him. The country to which he went had a food shortage and the son was starving. He was in trouble and needed help. He decided to ask his father to let him come back home, not as a son but as a hired man.

When the father saw his son, his love was so great that he felt *compassion* for him. He welcomed him home and planned a feast to celebrate his joy at his son's return.

Your parents feel this way about you. They love you, care for you, are concerned about you, and want to help when you need their support.

"The Parable of the Lost Son" teaches us about God's love. Our Heavenly Father loves us and has compassion for us. He understands our feelings, shares our hurts, and wants to help. Even though we sometimes make bad choices and live in a way that might not be good for us, He is ready to forgive us and welcome us when we turn to Him.

The Ten Virgins

(Matthew 25:1-13)

> Therefore keep watch, for you do not know the day or the hour.
> —Matthew 25:13

Object Needed: A diploma

Have you ever seen a diploma, or known anyone who has received one? A diploma is an important and treasured document. As you can see, this diploma has the name of the person to whom the diploma was presented and the name of a school, printed in beautiful letters on smooth white paper. It is enclosed in a leather case.

A diploma is given to someone who has met the requirements of a high school or college. It shows that the person has completed certain classes and courses of study and has passed the required tests. Many years of hard work are necessary to *prepare* to meet the requirements of a school and receive a diploma.

A college diploma indicates that the student has earned a degree. It gives special rights and privileges to that person. Teachers, nurses, accountants, pastors, doctors, lawyers, and dentists are some of the peole who have earned degrees and received diplomas. If you visit the office of one of these people you may see his diploma hanging on the wall. The degree gives him the rights and privileges to allow him to work at his profession. The diploma is given as a reward and an honor for his years of hard work.

43

Jesus used "The Parable of the Ten Virgins" to teach us about the importance of preparing to meet His requirements. "At that time the kingdom of heaven will be like ten virgins who took their lamps and went out to meet the bridegroom. Five of them were foolish and five were wise. The foolish ones took their lamps but did not take any oil with them. The wise, however, took oil in jars along with their lamps. The bridegroom was a long time in coming, and they all became drowsy and fell asleep.

"At midnight the cry rang out: 'Here's the bridegroom! Come out to meet him!'

"Then all the virgins woke up and trimmed their lamps. The foolish ones said to the wise, 'Give us some of your oil; our lamps are going out.'

"'No,' they replied, 'there may not be enough for both us and you. Instead, go to those who sell oil and buy some for yourselves.'

"But while they were on their way to buy the oil, the bridegroom arrived. The virgins who were ready went in with him to the wedding banquet. And the door was shut.

"Later the others also came. 'Sir! Sir!' they said. 'Open the door for us!'

"But he replied, 'I tell you the truth, I don't know you.'

"Therefore keep watch, because you do not know the day or the hour."

The requirements to be a Christian are simple. We must believe that Jesus is the Son of God and obey His commands. When we meet these requirements we are given the right and privilege to be God's children, and we receive the forgiveness of sins. The parable teaches us that we should live our lives in a way that is pleasing to God.

We can *prepare* ourselves to be loving Christians through prayer and by reading and studying the Bible. If we accept God's love we are prepared to love ourselves and others. The reward for our willingness to work and help others in Christian love is a satisfying feeling and the promise of eternal life. Christian work is a privilege and an honor!

44

The Persistent Widow

(Luke 18:1-8)

Will not God bring about justice for his chosen ones, who cry out to him day and night?
—Luke 18:7

Object Needed: Shoelace

The first shoes were pieces of bark, leaves, or leather tied to the bottom of feet with laces. About four hundred years ago a new style of shoe was worn that had side pieces and a tongue. Shoelaces were used to bring the sides of the shoe together.

Many of us today wear shoes that have shoelaces. If you are wearing shoes with laces, reach down and untie the shoelaces and retie them. Was it difficult?

When you were very young, you didn't know how to manage shoelaces—you had to learn. The way you learned was by practicing. At first it was probably difficult. Perhaps you had trouble making your fingers work as they should. To learn to tie shoelaces you had to be *persistent.* You didn't give up. You didn't get discouraged. You kept trying until you reached your goal. Now you can tie your shoelaces easily, almost without thinking about it. You can make the loops, fasten them tightly, and do it quickly. It's easy!

Christ told "The Parable of the Persistent Widow" to teach His disciples about *persistence.* He said, "In a certain town there was a judge who neither feared God nor cared about men. And there was a widow in that town who kept coming to him with the plea, 'Grant me justice against my adversary.'

"For some time he refused. But finally he said to himself, 'Even though I don't fear God or care about men, yet because this widow keeps bothering me, I will see that she

45

gets justice, so that she won't eventually wear me out with her coming!'

"And the Lord said, 'Listen to what the unjust judge says. And will not God bring about justice for his chosen ones, who cry out to him day and night? Will he keep putting them off? I tell you, he will see that they get justice, and quickly.' "

Christ told the story to show us that if an unjust judge would help the widow because she was persistent and didn't give up, how much more would God listen to His people and help them with their needs.

When we pray we should not become discouraged. We are instructed, in the Bible, "to always pray and not give up." God will treat us fairly and with love.

The Rich Fool

(Luke 12:13-21)

"You fool! This very night your life will be demanded from you." —Luke 12:20

Object Needed: Nuts, seeds, and cones; a picture of a chipmunk

Chipmunks are cute little animals that spend much of their time searching for food. Because they sleep most of the winter, they must gather seeds and nuts to use during that time. They live in underground burrows beneath rocks, tree roots, or old logs. Their homes are leaf-lined nests surrounded by storerooms.

Chipmunks have special pouches inside their cheeks, which they stuff with nuts or seeds. They carry the food to the storerooms and pile it up for later use. Although they sleep most of the winter, they wake up occasionally on a warm day, eat, and go back to sleep. Chipmunks need to *pile up and store* food so they can survive the cold time of the year.

"The Parable of the Rich Fool" is a story about a man who stored his crops in a greedy way. Jesus spoke to a crowd and told them this parable: "The ground of a certain rich man produced a good crop. He thought to himself, 'What shall I do? I have no place to store my crops.'

"Then he said, 'This is what I'll do. I will tear down my barns and build bigger ones, and there I will store all my grain and my goods. And I'll say to myself, 'You have plenty of good things laid up for many years. Take life easy; eat, drink and be merry.'

"But God said to him, 'You fool! This very night your life will be demanded from you. Then who will get what you have prepared for yourself?'

"This is how it will be with anyone who stores up things for himself but is not rich toward God."

The rich man had more than he needed or could ever use. His plans did not include God or other people. He was greedy and wanted to pile up all of his goods for himself. He gave no thought to other things that are important.

To be "rich toward God" we need to *pile up and store* spiritual qualities. As we spend time studying the Bible and consulting God through prayer, we learn what things in life are important. Learning about God's plan helps us use our time, money, and talents wisely. We may also learn how to understand and handle greed. God has an unlimited supply of love that He offers to us. If we accept His love and share it with others we become "rich toward God."